I0162547

Published by mad8 Publishing
Coldwater, Ontario

1

Canadian Cataloguing in Publication Data.

Fournier, Merci;
        Title: Plural Spaces

ISBN: 978-0-9685706-6-1

1. Fournier, Merci; 2. Poetry:

Merci Fournier

FRONT COVER:
Front cover photograph taken by the author.
Cover design and internal page design by Michelle Duff.

Plural Spaces

Merci Fournier

ACKNOWLEDGEMENTS

Some of the poems herein have appeared in the following publications:

Origins, CV11, University of Toronto Review, Nimbus Two, Canadian Author & Bookman, Waves, Rampike, Images, Poetry Australia, The Laughing Unicorn, (USA) Descant, Tide-pool,

Other Channels:

The Dry Wells of India (anthology), South Western Ontario chapbook "The Baker's Wedding".

Broadcast on CIXX FM, London.

Marzipan, Underwhich Editions.

To Cathy, Edie, Michelle, and of course, Chris.

The Summer I Was Twenty

The days were crimson and filled
with the ripeness of raspberry canes,
at dusk we swam in the Cherwell
black with shadows
and it seemed the nights
would hold us forever:

I still see ancient willows
bent over water and feel
hay stubble sharp against
my hand, but lately
my mind plays tricks and in
the tart aftertaste of youth
I no longer see your face.

Return

You showed me complacent parks
and stone stairways of the past
through Richmond, York and Warwick,
I left my touch to interweave with
ancient stone in undercrofts.
I'm drawn to the Yorkshires of my life
where farewells
are not to be looked at closely, only
left behind and not disturbed,
like mushrooms in the tender dark
where only you may check their course.

Threading Through Snarled Traffic

Black tonight making
scarlet tissue of old wounds
bare mouths expecting;
and there
          and there
are the favourite sore spots,
tonight by the water, threading
through the traffic of a season
aching for river beds
and topsy suns
tonight.

Tonight, the rehearsal, your
neck arched as the
waters
gather you in handfuls,

coming home,
through the snarled traffic.

Day One

You said 'I knew from day one',
and gave me images maximising
all I ever remembered about love.
You gave yourself, covering me with
long lost loves, the hidden meaning
working its way through my body,
your strong presence creeping into me
without my knowledge.
You have done this to me, a super nova
of moment some might say, perhaps
the last magic in my life, therefore
having honourable intent. I say I cannot
recall such lustre between two people,
the one intensifying the other,
all the bitterness flowing away
in that one last kiss.

The Pull Of You

You are the oldest stone
in my life, standing by me
through the centuries.
I've known of you for
many lives which indicate
the strength of you;

born together, knowing
the utmost, we've been
about the planet, our time
so ancient it occurred
before time began.

I'm beginning to understand
the pull of you, the thread
which holds me, the colossal
importance.

When Summer Comes

It is the day of obsession,
I am blind with fatigue and
still you bother with me,
it seems you are never through.
Today is the day I am spellbound:
you have bound my feet, ears,
encased my body in somebody else's
cadaver.

It is almost night time of this
very long day, I smell the jasmine
somewhere,   and you know my weakness
for flowers;
maybe, when summer comes, we'll
lean across the picnic table,
write white words to each other.

The Piano

We have a piano between us,
the scant sound musing me,
polishing plural spaces where
trills are born and much is made
of crescendo. I had
a love, a certain buoyancy, my
days decorated, believing the music
to be my own, darkest blue notes
providing my ears with sound of such
momentous movement
that my body became a vessel.

Perhaps I should pretend you're
inspiring me and in the trickle
of tune write myself a letter
telling what occurred that final
summer afternoon.

I have a piano with
mournful notes, my own
composition, hoping your
contribution lives on,
and that my finger tips
one blazing day will score
the fabric of our love.

Recognition

It's time
to end the subtlety,
give fresh credence
to ourselves,
rewards,
a time for gestures
to be translated
into formidable objects
like mountains and skulls;
have you forgotten
me?
I was here yesterday
at the bottom of your mind.

Forgiveness

Forgiveness is so unsure a thing,
right to the end we wring our hands
imitating Christ, or at least
trying to, the device old as time,
years slipping like a worn silk cloak
but discovering past events still
clinging as though distracted infants
unable to find a breast.
There's this urgency, now
on a daily basis that
the wicked shears will chop at anything,
my past being deleted one day
at a time, and the ghosts of one's life
indicating it never really occurred.
Each night I look at the stars,
more brilliant than ever, knowing
one small slip and that cosmic wind
will scoop me up, return me
to my ancestors.

Indications

This love is sour
in my mouth,
roots of trees
infiltrate my head
which is why
I shake it
wave my hands
in your direction,
why it is hard for me
to see you because of this
sheet of blood that hangs
between us.
There have been indications
your wall is softening
but the roots in my head
are almost at my eyes,
oh love

plant a bird in my branches
this day.

Passage Of Time

The golden years were when you sat with me
and held my hand,
together we jumped across the moon and
into ourselves again.
When the clouds had gone from my eyes
you too had disappeared.
The ground beneath us now is peppered with
spent acorns and my hands are lined
with gnarled thoughts, but still, for you
I'd bend myself in two.

This Outback

Because you have touched
all my places your arms
have become my country;
you lament because I have swept
your face, felt tight borders
hugging your sides.
You have chosen this outback
of emotion and the churches
of your head swing back,
their bells counting hours
your knees rocking as you try
to remember its lullaby.

Remembering

The nights are lonely now
as we settle into our last
quarter, but still, my dear
we must remember those
times we held each other
close, forehead to forehead
and the nights were full
of strange magic and fine
talk; it really was us
and in our battered chest
of time we lift the garments
one by one, shaking them well.

What I Do Now

In my house they're laying
new carpet while I drift
through their day; this is now
what I do: photograph
my neighbour's rose bush
the one with the deepest scent
imaginable because it's old as myself.
I remember those deep dark days,
all blooms having their own
signature,
remembering is what I now do.

This Is Why

Because we have to begin
somewhere because the raging
sandstorm starts with a twist
of wind, because of you and the day
of meeting, this is why.

In autumn sounds bear
a different resonance,
apart from changed light
causing the tearing of
sad places, a banquet of pain;
this is why.

In your beginning, the
mightiest sensation, suddenly
there, the bridal chamber
decorated with goodness
and all the birds of the universe
at our wedding.

This is why I'm fond of
this deep distraction
causing a *frisson* of memory,
life not being the same
without you.

Tamara Said

'silently wonderful,' you said
of my cat, orange bulk
his own property.
You know all about love
and its fixture, how time
really doesn't heal and how
unexpectedly the soft
leap of an animal proffers
some understanding.

We are individuals who
having walked the long
plank of separation
require at least the touch
of connection that only
an animal can give.

Seeing For The First Time

In the lake of choice we
air problems, sit on lake
bottom, it is presumptuous
to assume all is well.
For centuries this lake
has known tranquility,
darkest corners biblical,
stangers allude to an area
of defence,   all this
stuffed into a cracker bottom
boat, stealing the lake's larder
bone by bone.

We have handicapped the lake's
reserve, cracked open its face
dubbing in words we could not
utter. The lake has become a placebo
shared between us, a gun
or rocket that hits our
eyes;
seeing for the first time.

A Space Odyssey

A silence like no
other silence, deep
within the birth and
death of planets,
taking hold in seconds
but in reality, millennia.
A silence where a
cathedral's sound in
the dead of night
is deafening; this peace
where the order of
self is established,
the stars simple
way stations; this
is the peace beyond
understanding, the
cataclysmic event
that is death,
enabling a perspective,
this is the familiar.

Cosmos

In swirling gases, galaxies perform
pre-timed mazurkas
the wonderful ploughing match
in the sky, calling bans of marriage
through the borealis.

In Lapland the reindeer alerts himself,
hearing sounds of life's beginnings
language of stars in
every nova,
                    hears
every hair of his coat
sing its own song.

Michelle

In the house by the lake
you have woven a dream,
a victory, all the squares
and rounds fused in a
subtlety you never imagined.
In the darker shades of recall
animal soft reached to comfort
and sustain, your dearest reward
being simplicity.

In the house by the lake
you have woven a dream,
the stars being of your own keeping.

Angiogram

hospital corridor
the long wait, where words scatter
among chrome carcass of stretchers: new
features in your life.

machine gun clacking dye injects, writhes
into you finding truth,
black cross common marker at
your midriff means
another frame and burst
red-hot liquid
bullying about your head;

behind glass, we watch robot flying
fingers of dye.
on the high altar of table
hammering machine pinpoints
the massive architecture of disease.

My Mother Is Leaving

thorn in my side mother
will depart   leaving
my jig-a-jig life to me;
sewn into compartments
in my body, when I feel movement
it is her.

blood of old wounds
a part of me my mother my
imperfections   and I
have grown to
love them, my mother
is leaving

tearing herself out of me
like an old bandage

A Planetary Shift

They're talking of web sites
and dot com, could be some
other language, invention.
The top of my desk covered
by words seems antiquated
yet comforting, like people
buying old lamps.
I hold a certain grudge
against technology, this
ocean of info without
pull of tide,
I have an idea
of words becoming art,
moving exhibitions of some
archaic activity, and all
the viewers rigid, their minds
coded and controlled and us
old people pushing ourselves
farther and farther off the
planet.

Beach

You are sitting on a navy blue
beach, it is summer and children
are all around you:
you have arrived at the other end
of the world and have words
dripping from your fingers.

I ask you about your husband
and your eyes swim like vacant lots,
'it is enough' you say, and there are
blue eyes hidden in the bottom of your purse.

You live on the beach in a house
and the slots of ideas
come rapidly, you collect them all
lay them in old boxes
tending them as you would children.

                Now and then
a hand reaches out
strokes your forehead,
                as if amazed
at how you left him
on a beach at the back of your mind.

Two Women In A Glass Garden

Your eyes are a curious blue; we've
been introduced and there's something
in your pattern, my ears have picked up
something   maybe the way your cheek
curves, the telling lines.
After lunch we stroll in the garden,
should be a unifying experience, yet
there are your eyes, edging me.

We sit in the empty gazebo, again this
chameleon look, your secrets circumvented,
and you tell me I am steeped in guilt. It is
your eyes again, this band of blue running
through the seam of you, as though I walk
in a glass garden.

Lunch hour seeps into afternoon
the blue of you prevails,
and in the oblivion of words you sink your teeth
into my afternoon,
into the canny knowledge of women.

Photograph

you show me
boats at grey dawn
like atlantic dowagers,
I begin to see why
you were drawn to
this particular harbour
where masts are shaky signatures
on brown water;
I look deep into this
photo with its ghostly
overtones and promises

and when you tell me
how sad a week it was
I understand why you were
able to focus
so minutely.

After Reading An Account Of Torture

Evil has arrived. Right now
I don't know who I am,
years I've waited, knowing
it was coming: "evil" I'm talking of.
Beaten feet, anal rape, a mouse
released into a woman's vagina;
what *have* we become? More than I
expected, this is like tearing out
the tongues of singing larks.
We have descended to the ultimate
scream.

If this is how we are,
an appalling capacity for cruelty,
then why the beauty of a landscape
the lapping of oceans, the constant
waves of energy when one falls
in love?

All The Reasons

Our father's first illness unwrapped
itself around us children
spoke its icy words somewhere
above our heads. We lay
in the blister of night like small prunes
saturated with sayings from the
cook's gypsy friends who lurked in the
backs of our minds like shadows;
we watched the gardener build his empire,
he too had his illnesses chasing us
into dreams, old men before our
time, and behind the hen coops we
smashed eggs, watching the rich yolk
pour out and sculpt the long grass
agreeably.
Our dreams were our world, making up
for sentimentality, all the reasons we would
die for, eventually.

His Last Season

In the brown garden herbaceous borders
bloom in their last spate, hors d'oeuvre of
spring tucked into root systems.
Next month winds will cross the marsh
into father's last season, roadways of his body
snarled.
Picking flints, father heaves barrow loads,
he's that determined.
Later he'll sip homeopathic remedies
from bottles lined the way a woman
stores preserves, mother raving insults
as he leaves a heavy trail of garlic
through each room.

One Snowy Day In April

Winter is upon us and
I feel cave stirrings
in my body, a need for
closer ties: there's this
warning that perhaps
this is the last winter, not
enough food provided, not
enough of everything because
you have passed out of my
daylight into some perfect
order leaving all the winters
mine.

Homecoming

Today the michaelmas daisies
signify another year almost done;
Father's home now, incoherent
he shuffles through our minds
impeding his own activities, wife
become primitive parent;
she has guessed his days
in the dreadful immobility
of face.
Throughout the small kitchen
kettle in hand he searches
in vain, only the dog
making contact.

The Day Of The Sunken Garden

The day my father was
buried, lowered into his
sunken garden, world
turned black in my hand;
service brief, what was there
to say in a lifetime
of pencil scratchings?
Flies buzzed in the church
that Saturday morning, life
careening toward this moment,
this lowering.

Father taught me
to remove shoots
from tomatoes, taught
that women were loving
and allowed to be so,

the day of my father's funeral
trumpets should have sounded
and the world dimmed
to impossible darkness.

The Last Train

You watch the trains go by
as though they were black corpses,
beat time
as if it is your heart
and not your fingers driving against
the railing.
An assortment of signals
enters your brain as you recall
the last train out of Poland;
you prefer not to look back
because all trains have cattle cars
hidden in their interiors, and because
you have promised yourself never
to presume anything again.

The Gentleman Farmer

It's been a good season
red apples stowed away,
and what does the gentleman farmer
feel about the rest of the world?
He touches perimeters
feels rims:
strange things have happened, like the night
he fell off the planet, stars clenched
between his teeth.

The farmer is a gentleman
rat traps in his pocket,
makes lists of all the grand operas in the world;
he has a very large shopping bag.

Dispute

You argue about black textiles
whether the roofing man will arrive,
you seize the failures, the park bench misfortunes
and force them into bottles.
You wear stars to mark the occasion

a lark flies out of your mouth

Dice

you roll the dice
the miraculous combination,
the glandular episode that
ends with the two of us
locked into photographs of
shanghai, the smell of old wood.
you roll the dice twice, hold them
against your mouth

they click in your hands like bones.

The Performance

We are in a circus tent, the applause
is deafening,
my mother and father enter the ring
on unicycles, their machines garlanded.
They perform a parody of their lives,
in the end the cycles are in pieces
and my parents are fused together;
it all happens very swiftly.
After each performance a janitor
sweeps the debris,
everybody cheers him, but he never
raises his head.
There are two performances each day,
I have never missed one.

Old Barns

Torn timber, forgotten
in a farmer's field,
no secrets or proud moments now;
birth and death have felt your touch, and
on moonlit nights ghosts flit through
for remembrance;
only the lilacs have survived, their
fragrance permeates each gentle board
settling memories.

Edge Of Season, East Anglia

Cloud swings low through windswept marsh
toward night
and rain-birds moderate harsh cries to
plummet rod-like in perpetual baptism;
estuary cats prowl carefully among
dismembered boats, while
out to sea, fishermen light endless
cigarettes and angry, toss them
overboard to think of Saturday night's
rosy limbs;

this desolate coast
                    halts
for a moment
at the bottom of a winter,
and I catch it, maybe once
in a lifetime.

Bone Structure There In The Sky

They scream in the sky, it is
part of the bird, they wheel
one on the other, ancient bone structures
right there in the sky,
bird and the feathers are singular things
the moment all feathered and the
beak of the bird so wide
as it swoops and defines itself
right in the sky;
its beak is open and the wild part
of the bird is singing, the last part
of the world

and every wild thing there is

Ice Being So Pure

Ice, (such a miracle), slow ice
forming its myriad pattern,
an unfolding sequence revealing
excellence of centuries, and now
I hold it, hearing the stillness of
creation. Such creatures in this mix,
the throb of watery hearts singing
their deep song, each taking its turn
on this vast miraculous planet, blue
space into ice, into the bluer depths
of concealment.

Tide

The great grey ocean
with its marvellous eye
feeling for tide-pull;
saltboard the way
I remember during that
unkempt childhood of
no harmony, the steady
sea heart heard
a long way off as
a child's first cries
passage the water.
The shale is wet today,
all night winds have
crossed and re-crossed
that sea with its
odious depths; we also
are pulled this other way,
tide sensing saline
within us, that great
precursor of us all.

From A Ship's Balcony

The catch and pull of
night ocean: a momentous depth
and myself not quite certain
of its power, except beyond
the spray, a black curtain
and a different tempo of drift.
I stood, that night, wind almost
hissing, feeling the tug of
ocean, imagining so nearly
of falling into the blackening
cauldron with its herds of
unknown creature; and I thought
of that continent of which I
know nothing, except its
sepulchral undertones amidst
the keening wind, and remembering
most of all having to pull myself
away, the force being that persuasive.

This Fine-Looking Man

Drug disabled he turns himself in
to the nearest hospital, whispers
he can't go on like this any more
and on the corridor stretcher
he meets the end of the world.
He will start on Librium,
walking in and out of himself
as the bastard years button him
down, insidious magnet of drug
drawing him backwards into
the rush of white fever,
psychiatrist opening him
on a blinding knife edge.

Merci Fournier

Merci Fournier was born and raised in England, coming to Alberta, Canada, to continue her career as a registered nurse. She married an RCAF pilot, settled in Ontario, and had two sons. In her early forties, Merci began to write, and had poetry published in Canada, the U.S., and Australia. Recently, Merci moved to Stratford, ON.